GOING VIRAL

Lessons in Free to Low Cost Online Marketing

Corwin Smith

DEDICATION

I would like to all the small business owners who like myself comprise the backbone of American business, who struggle through the good, the bad and the ugly to provide economic life for themselves, their families and ultimately our entire nation. Live long and prosper much!

This book entitled: "**<u>Going Viral: Lessons in Free to Low Cost Online Marketing</u>**" is the sole and exclusive property of the Author. This book shall not be reproduced in whole or in part whether written or reproduced in any other manner known or unknown to exist, without the written and/or express permission of the author and/or publishing company.

<u>DISCLAIMER</u>: This book is meant to aid you in your pursuit of growing your business. I would like to make it absolutely clear this book (*or any other book in and of itself*) will not guarantee overnight success. Like anything else in life, rewarding results are obtained and/or improved upon by continual effort, study, patience, discipline, determination & hard work. As such individual results will vary.

<u>LEGAL NOTICE</u>: This book provides the names of many companies, all of which are the exclusive property of their respective owners. The listing of these names are in no way intended as an endorsement, promotion or infringement upon the intellectual rights of their respective owners.

<u>NOTE</u>: I tried to include only websites that are free or cost very little. As such, many of the websites I've listed are indeed free. However, in a attempt to offer you [small business AND/OR website owner] additional resources, I also included some helpful websites that require fees of some sort to patronize their services/products. These listings are by no means all inclusive. There are always new sites popping up regularly. So expect to see more added in future editions.

<u>Requirements</u>: The following is the few and simple things you will need to gain the most from the use of this book.

A Computer with an internet connection

Time Management Skills (*the time that will be required to actually sit down and sign up or create accounts at many of these websites*).

A Willingness to Follow Through (*by this I mean the tenacity to sit down and sign up or create a account for each and every website listed [or as many as you deem useful for your particular needs] when time permits, hint . . . time management!*).

TABLE OF CONTENTS

NOTE: I make every attempt to keep the listings within this book current and up to date. However, we all know unfortunately businesses/websites come and go. So if any of the listings provided are out of service or incorrect and you catch it before I do, I welcome you letting me know. You can email me at **cs@396designs.com**

In the Subject Line of Your Email Please Put:

[GV Listings Correction]

ACKNOWLEDGMENTS

I would like to acknowledge as well as thank the entire staff of CreateSpace.com for making the printing/publishing of this book possible. You guys are a God send to starving authors. I would also like to acknowledge as well as thank all the business owners who purchased this book and made it such a useful reference in the realm of online [as well as offline] marketing and advertising.

About this Book

You've taken a step in the right direction by purchasing this book. This alone shows your level of dedication toward seeing your business a success. Both of which are an action and a character to be admired. I wish this book to be a GOD send in your every endeavor.

Without spending to much time ranting about statistics of how the web has grown and the overwhelming number of websites that can help business or website owners grow, I would just like to use this section entitled, "*about this book*" to explain how this book reads as well as how best to apply its contents to help grow your business. That being said . . .

This book is categorized into three sections, which are entitled, "*Did we say FREE?*" , "*Additional Resources*" and "Bonus Resources". The "free" section is a listing of predominantly free websites which include such websites as auction, social, business-to-business networking, video and picture sharing websites to name but a few.

The "additional" section is organized into a diverse listing of very useful resources for any business and/or website owner looking to maximize his/her entrepreneurial efforts. The last section entitled, "Bonus Resources" is a NEW section rich with advice, tips, strategies and tactics on growing your business through both online as well as offline means.

Lastly, but of dire importance is the action needed to best use the information (*i.e. the websites*) exposed within this book. Since there is a vast number of websites listed within this book, one must realistically know this is clearly not an overnight task (*i.e. the creating of accounts, viewing/ browsing from site to site, etc.*).

That being said, one will need to exhibit more than just a little patience and tenacity. For most this should not come at all as a surprise since running a business requires these attributes among many others. However, for those few of you who tire early, know this, "when you are about to consider quitting, your competitors will be pushing full steam ahead". Endurance and perseverance are but two of the ingredients that separate the successful from the mediocre. So it boils down to a matter of "how bad do you want it".

With that said, I suggest pacing yourself. Everything has a method to it, and this is no exception. Below I've listed a few time management techniques to help you get the most from this book.

Try and set aside at least 2 hours a day for browsing, signing up and creating an account for a minimum number of websites. (*Of course the hours and number of websites will vary based on your own particular situation, circumstances and patience*).

If you run a tight schedule, then add an extra one half to one hour to your morning wake up or before going to bed. If this still doesn't seem to be a viable option for you then go hard on the weekends (*i.e. Friday night, several times a day Saturday/Sunday, etc.*). The bottom line is you have to make time for it or you've surrendered to defeat before even giving yourself a shot.

Since signing up for these websites means more usernames and passwords, (*I know just when most of us are already inundated with usernames and passwords*) I suggest creating a systematic naming strategy. As far as usernames go, many require your email to be your username, for those that don't try using some variation of your business' name, gist, colors, etc. Password naming however, doesn't afford that luxury. So I have provided a few example naming strategies.

Since many of the websites listed have short names, try using their name with a name and/or number of your own. (*Examples: myspace360, facebookjayjay, diggtommygun56, etc.*).

BY ALL MEANS, resist the urge to use the same password for all websites. Although, convenient, its not safe or practical. If by chance someone finds out your password for one site, then you'll regret that short lived and disastrous convenience. So **DON'T DO IT**!

If you're the hard head type, and you insist on using the same password, then at least add a different number to each one (*Example: facebooksamepassword001, myspacesamepassword002, etc.*). Just be sure to keep a copy of your numbering system incase you forget which number belongs to which site.

Lastly, if this section missed you by a long shot, you will always have the option to reset your password with their "*forgot your password*" option. Without any more dragging, I would again like to congratulate you for taking that extra step in your quest for growing your business.

Read on young grasshopper!

CHAPTER 1
AUCTION WEBSITES

Unless you've been living in outer space for the last 13 years or so, then you have most certainly heard of e-bay and Amazon. Without question, these are two of the biggest self serving auction/seller websites on the web (*if not thee biggest*).

What many of us don't know however is the fact that there are many more such sites offering similar services and just like their behemoth forerunners many are free to sign up or create an account. For the most part all charge a small percentage of your sales price. In any event they can be a very powerful tool to those individuals or businesses that choose to sell their products by means of an auction. All are free to register, but charge a nominal fee to sell.

<u>Pros</u>:

Since the owners of these websites spend most of their efforts trying to build traffic to the website, their marketing efforts actually work for you, which means this doubles up on your own marketing efforts. Not a bad deal considering the minimum (*i.e. a percentage of your sales*) investment involved.

<u>Cons</u>:

Since chances are whatever you're selling or re-selling their will definitely be others selling it as well, your competition will often be fierce. Don't fret or waiver though, because it is still worth posting your goods/services rather than not.

www.AmazonServices.com (*amazon's auction site*)

www.E-Bay.com (*for those of you who aren't listed*)

www.Bid4Assets.com

www.BidStart.com (*geared toward antiques*)

www.Bidz.com (*predominantly jewelry*)

www.Christies.com (*geared toward high ticket items*)

www.Cqout.com (*UK based but still US operative - $3 to register*)

www.ECrater.com

www.Etsy.com

www.Ha.com (*geared toward collectibles*)

www.OnlineAuction.com (*$8/month*)

www.Playle.com (*free to register*)

www.Webstore.com

www.Webidz.com (*$5 to register*)

www.wensy.com

www.Skinnerinc.com (*geared toward high ticket items*)

www.Sothebys.com (*geared toward high ticket items*)

www.UBid.com

Remember these websites can prove very lucrative, profitable and rewarding for certain products you may be selling or even considering selling as well.

CHAPTER 2
BLOG WEBSITES

Blogs are very useful tools for any thriving business. A clever way to not only spread the word about your business and/or website, but also a subtle way of gathering input about your business and/or website from users and potential customers alike. With many of today's exposure websites (*i.e.* *Facebook, MySpace, etc.*) offering such services, it's often hard to distinguish between blog only websites and these. However, there are quite a few websites dedicated exclusively or predominantly to blog functionality. As such, I chose to list only these in particular for this section.

www.Blogster.com

www.Blogger.com

www.My.Opera.com (*www.my.opera.com*)

www.Presently.com

www.Tumblr.com

www.Twitter.com

www.Xanga.com

www.Yammer.com

www.Weebly.com

www.WordPress.com

www.DropJack.com

www.Fwisp.com

www.Gabbr.com

www.Posterous.com

www.TypePad.com (*min. $8.95/month*).

www.OpenDiary.com

www.Jisko.com

www.Identi.ca

www.Numpa.com

NOTE: Some of these websites also offer services as that of those listed within the social networking websites section. Also some of the aforementioned sites aren't technically blog sites as they are bookmarking sites with blogging functionality.

CHAPTER 3
BOOKMARK WEBSITES

Bookmark websites are also a definite asset in your arsenal to grow your business and/or build traffic for your website. They are unique in that they tend to offer a dual benefit.

On the one hand they serve as a means to keep you organized in respect to having access to all your favorite websites wherever you are (*on or off the road*).

On the other hand since most allow other account members to view others favorite bookmarks and often rate them, this gives you the advantage of posting your own website to your bookmark list, which in turn makes your website accessible/viewable to other account members. But best of all most of these bookmark sites are absolutely free, and who doesn't like free!

www.Delicious.com

www.Plaxo.com

www.StumbleUpon.com

www.Digg.com

www.Reddit.com

www.Mixx.com

www.Fark.com

www.FriendFeed.com

www.Clipmarks.com

www.Newsvine.com

www.Diigo.com

www.Propeller.com

www.Mister-Wong.com

www.DZone.com

www.BlinkList.com

www.Faves.com

www.Simpy.com

www.OneView.com

www.Ping.fm

www.WebWag.com

www.HelloTxt.com

www.Squidoo.com

CHAPTER 4
BUSINESS TO BUSINESS WEBSITES

Business to business websites some times referred to as B2B websites will probably offer the most promise for most business and/or website owners. These are the ideal platforms for individuals just like you to build mutually benefiting relationships with business and/or website owners like yourself. These websites are also a great place to learn more about your particular industry (*often times from veterans in your specialty*).

Many of these websites often serve as calendar boards, if you will, of upcoming events that are usually related to offline networking functions like meetings, seminars, etc. catering to nearly every industry and specialty. Attending some of the events can only prove to help spread awareness for your business and/or website, not to mention broaden your knowledge about your industry. By all means take full advantage!

www.BigTent.com

www.Biznik.com

www.CoFoundr.com (*no misspelling, there is no "e"*)

www.EFactor.com

www.Ecademy.com

www.EConnect.Entrepreneur.com

www.FastPitchNetworking.com

www.Gather.com

www.JaseZone.com

www.LinkedIn.com

www.NetworkingForProfessionals.com

www.PatnerUp.com

www.PerfectBusiness.com

www.Ryze.com

www.StartUpNation.com

www.TalkBizNow.com

www.UpSpring.com

www.Xing.com

www.Yelp.com

www.YoungEntrepreneur.com

www.Ziggs.com

CHAPTER 5
ONLINE CLASSIFIED WEBSITES

A lot has changed since the internet's inception and widespread growth. Particularly, the idea of classified advertising as it was once perceived. The term now includes the reference to its online counterpart. Very much like its' offline sibling, online classifieds offer an inexpensive way of selling an unlimited number of things, be it products and/or services.

However, differing from its offline counterpart, online classified advertisements are usually without to little cost. Unfortunately this inexpensive attribute often comes with a price. Since they are usually free, they are often overpopulated which can sometimes make it hard for some items to be viewed or even sold for that matter.

There are however both exceptions and variations to this common disadvantage. One such exception is Craigslist. And the biggest variation will be what you are selling. The more unique (*as well as the cheaper*) your sell item(s) are the more attention they are likely to receive.

In any event, given both the good and the bad of classifieds, they are still worthy of use. So don't be discouraged, they often help to make for a well balanced marketing regimen. Because there are literally thousands of free classified websites I chose to only list the ones that are more widely known and actually used.

www.Craigslist.org

www.BackPage.com

www.Classifieds1000.com

www.EBayClassifieds.com (*formerly Kijiji Classifieds*)

www.Hoobly.com

www.Oodle.com

www.UsFreeAds.com

CHAPTER 6
PHOTO SHARING WEBSITES

As the old adage goes, "a picture is worth a thousands words", can literally hold real significance in today's world of business, particularly when it comes to doing business online. People tend to be moved and more entertained by visual stimuli. This can be unquestionably evidenced by our growing obsession with interactive websites, applications and software.

So there is no wonder that there is a proliferation of websites offering the ability to upload, edit and share photos to not only friends, but to the entire world as well, is on the rise. Initially many of these websites had primarily social (*non-commercial*) tones. That has and continues to change though. Many are opening their doors to business members, which is definitely a plus for any thriving business and/or website owner.

With photo sharing websites, you can harness the power of visual stimuli and showcase photos of your company's products, inventions, designs, etc. for the entire world to take notice.

www.PhotoBucket.com

www.DailyBooth.com

www.Flickr.com

www.Fotolog.com

www.Sneppi.com

www.Flukiest.com

CHAPTER 7
SOCIAL WEBSITES

Social websites (*followed by marketplace websites*) make up the bulk of the listings contained in this book. This is primarily because they out number all other categories. Social websites although originally intended for just what their name implies, socializing, have traversed leaps and bounds in terms of their use and popularity.

Once used as a means of meeting new people and staying in touch with both distant and close friends alike, social websites have evolved into world reaching networking platforms that transcend beyond industries, borders, cultures and nationalities to name but a few.

More entertaining and often less expensive than a long distance phone call, social sites offer a host of benefits that can help grow nearly any business both big and small. What makes them a taste more powerful than many of the other websites listed in this book is the fact that they offer more functionality combined into one account.

You can often chat, post/blog, share photo/video content and even access all this functionality from your mobile phone. And in today's fast moving, hard hitting, down to the millisecond world we live in this is definitely an asset for any one trying to expand the reach of their brand, company, opportunities, products and/or services, etc.

Many of the social websites we've listed here are indeed social sites, however many of them allow you to create and edit a profile, which opens the door for you to promote whatever it is you're promoting (*be it yourself, your proposition, your company, etc.*) which is what this book is all about. However, some may restrict commercial postings, so for those that do I recommend referencing your promotion as your means of employment (*i.e. as your employer*) and make it your job to creatively include a link (*active or not*), a brief statement, etc. about what it is your promoting.

www.DipDive.com

www.connect.aim.com

www.arto.com

www.Badoo.com

www.Bebo.com

www.BlackPlanet.com

www.Buzz.com

www.Facebook.com

www.FourSquare.com

www.Friendster.com

www.Fubar.com

www.GlobalGrind.com

www.Gravee.com

www.Hi5.com

www.Hotklix.com

www.HoverSpot.com

www.Jaiku.com

www.Last.fm

www.LifeKnot.com

www.Lunch.com

www.Lynki.com

www.MeetUp.com

www.Migente.com

www.MocoSpace.com

www.Mulitply.com

www.MyLife.com

www.MySpace.com

www.Neo.org

www.En.Netlog.com

www.NetVIbes.com

www.Orkut.com *(owned by Google)*

www.PageFlakes.com

www.Parlus.com

www.PerfSpot.com

www.Piczo.com

www.Planypus.us

www.Plurk.com

www.Qlipso.com

www.QuaterLife.com

www.Reunion.com

www.ShoutLife.com

www.SkyRock.com

www.Sonico.com

www.Tagged.com

www.Viadeo.com

www.Virb.com

www.Vyoom.com

www.Uk.Wasabi.com

www.Yazzem.com

www.LiveMocha.com *(language learning social network)*

www.MyYearBook.com

www.Ning.com

www.Bolt.com

www.FledgeWing.com

www.MeetIn.org

www.Tribe.net

www.Buzz.Yahoo.com

www.BrightKite.com

www.YouAre.com

www.PeopleSound.com

www.Hictu.com

www.BeeMood.com

NOTE: Many of these websites also offer services as that of those listed within the blog websites section.

CHAPTER 8
VIDEO SHARING WEBSITES

Videos have become a very powerful and driving force in today's world of online marketing and advertising. This can be evidenced by the fact that YouTube alone averages way more than a thousand videos uploaded or downloaded a day (*and this is being modest to say the least*). Couple that with the fact that YouTube was (*and still is*) such a huge phenomenon that the online behemoth Google purchased it. What makes it even more phenomenal is the fact that it is completely free (*for now*) and that is definitely a GOD Send for business owners the world over.

Since traditional television commercials can and often are expensive, not to mention limited in reach (*globally speaking*), online videos offer a considerably less expensive alternative that is very much accessible to most business and/or website owners. This is powerful! Think about it, with minimum requirements (*i.e. camcorder, some video editing software, etc.*) you can create, edit and post your very own brand commercial on YouTube as well as a number of other similar websites for the entire world to potentially see.

This section alone should prove valuable to most business and/or website owners looking for that extra edge, when it comes to gaining brand exposure.

www.Blip.tv

www.Blip.fm

www.Camyoo.com

www.DailyMotion.com

www.Flixster.com

www.Stickam.com

www.Video.TurnHere.com

www.VideoEgg.com

www.Vimeo.com

www.VSocial.com

www.YouTube.com

www.Zooppa.com

www.Wistia.com

www.MotionBox.com

www.BrightCove.com

www.ClipShack.com

www.LiveVideo.com

www.Revver.com

www.SelfCast.com

www.UVouch.com

www.PixelFish.com

www.Viddler.com

www.VidiLife.com

www.Zoopy.com

www.Veoh.com

www.WebShots.com

www.VodPod.com

NOTE: Some of these websites also offer similar services (*i.e.* *uploading/downloading of photos as well*) as that of those listed within the photo sharing websites.

CHAPTER 9
E-MARKETING WEBSITES N' MORE

As intended this book is all about helping you grow your business both free and inexpensively. So this section is a helpful plus, if you will. Many of the websites or companies listed in this section aren't necessarily free but they do however cost less than what you might think. For example, there are many within this section that will allow you to send as many as 5000 marketing e-mails monthly for less than $20 a month. So with that in mind I have provided a nice listing for your benefit.

Some of the websites in this section are completely free and on top of that will pay you (*or the advertiser they represent will*) for allowing advertisements to be placed on your website. Not a bad trade off at all. Others offer other useful business related services.

www.247RealMedia.com

www.AdBrite.com

www.AdReady.com

www.CJ.com (*one of the best affiliate program providers on the web*)

www.ConstantContact.com

www.MyEmma.com

www.Email.ExactTarget.com

www.Google.com (*Adwords, Adsense, etc.*)

www.YellowPages.com

 www.MadMimi.com

www.GraphicMail.com

www.VerticalResponse.com

www.StreamSend.com

www.EmailBrain.com

www.JangoMail.com

www.GetResponse.com

www.IContact.com (*www.icontact.com*)

www.Jivox.com

www.Kontera.com

www.Yesmail.com

www.AWeber.com

www.BenchmarkEMail.com

www.Campaigner.com

www.PinPointe.com

www.WhoIsBusinessListings.com

CHAPTER 10
ONLINE PRESS RELEASE SERVICES WEBSITES

Not given as much attention as they deserve, press releases can be powerful tools in your overall marketing efforts. Although, there is more than just writing a few paragraphs about a product, service or idea to writing successful press releases, they can however prove to be very beneficial in getting the word out about your promotion.

In any event, I have included several websites that allow you to post or submit, if you will, your press release. And they in turn will make it available for a host of media outlets both online as well as off. What makes most of these websites I listed even more valuable is the fact that most of them are free, that's right that word we all love again . . . FREE, FREE, FREE!

www.1888PressRelease.com

www.FreePressRelease.com

www.I-NewsWire.com (*www.i-newswire.com*)

www.NewsWireToday.com

www.PRLog.org

www.PR.com

www.PRFree.com

www.PRWeb.com

www.Send2Press.com

CHAPTER 11
ONLINE MARKETPLACE WEBSITES

I'm not done with you yet young grasshopper. Another huge but often overlooked or simply unknowingly neglected channel for marketing and promoting your business online is the ever growing segment of online market portals or places. Popping up all over the web and with much success, these marketing instruments offer huge potential for business and website owners (*big and small alike*).

Differing from other websites listed in this book, market place websites are designed for exactly what you need them to be for . . . creating a place where you can make real time sales from your products and/or services. Of course there is usually a fee (*usually small often in the form of a commission*), but worth it if you have merchandise to move. However, many I have listed here are . . . yeah, you guessed it! They're FREE!

Some of the websites I listed are what we would deem "specialty or niche" market place websites. Many offering the ability to sale everything from horses, event tickets (*i.e. concerts, sporting events, etc.),* to antiques, art, CD's/DVD's, textbooks and even second hand items, to name but a few. So there is pretty much a market for nearly all readers of this book.

www.AbeBooks.com

www.AgriSeek.com

www.Alibaba.com

www.ArtFire.com

www.AtomicMall.com

www.BluJay.com

www.Bonanzle.com

www.Buy.com

www.CafePress.com

www.CoastToCoastTickets.com

www.Collect.com

www.CyberAttic.com

www.En.Dawanda.com

www.ECampus.com

www.Equine.com

www.EquineNow.com

www.EquipmentTradeerOnline.com

www.Shops.GoDaddy.com

www.GoAntiques.com

www.Google.com (*the merchant center*)

www.Half.EBay.com (*an EBay co.*)

www.NewEggMall.com

www.PayPal-Shopping.scom

www.PetClassifieds.us (*I know, it could have been listed in e-classifieds*)

www.Powells.com

www.Sedo.com

www.RubyLane.com

www.SecondSpin.com

www.Sell.com

www.ShopHandMade.com

www.StubHub.com

www.TextbooksRUs.com

www.Tias.com

www.TripleClicks.com

www.Trocadero.com

www.Wigix.com

www.E-Junkie.com

www.HorseClicks.com

www.HorseTopia.com

www.Ioffer.com (*www.ioffer.com*)

www.Liquidation.com

www.MadeItMyself.com (*www.madeitmyself.com*)

www.Luxury.Malleries.com (*luxury items*)

www.Apps.Facebook.com/marketplace/

www.FiveRR.com (*www.fiverr.com – two "r"'s*)

www.fivesquids.co.uk

www.GigMe5.com

www.Fourerr.com

www.TenBux.com

www.Outsourcerr.com

www.GigBucks.com

www.TeleGigz.com

www.JustaFive.com

www.Dollar3.com

www.JobsFor10.com

www.Twentyville.com

www.Fittytown.com

www.Hundoville.com

www.Zeerk.com

www.UpHype.com

CHAPTER 12
SEO SERVICES WEBSITES

The websites listed within this section are geared toward Search Engine Optimization (*more commonly referred to as SEO*) Services. Although, SEO services are diverse in respect to the available options one has when patronizing these services ythere are several aspects to SEO, such as search engine submission services, "key word" or "meta tag" services, superior sitemap development, and the list goes on. However, to keep it rather simple and to the point of inexpensively growing your business through the use of online marketing, I have elected to only list websites that offer search engine submission services (*although some offer more services*).

And to keep pace with the book's gist of FREE, most the following SEO services websites are indeed just that (*at least their search engine submission services are*).

www.BuildTraffic.com

www.SearchEngineBlaster.com

www.AddPro.com

www.AddMe.com

www.Submission-Pro.com

www.SubmitExpress.com

www.MegaWebPromotion.com (*primarily fee based services - but one of the best*)

Also keep in mind that you can manually submit your website in most cases for free directly to the major search engines, directories and/or metacrawlers (i.e. yahoo, google, msn/bing, ask, etc.) without much challenge in doing so.

To do so simply search "submit my website" within their search tools [boxes] or see some of the links I have provided below. Here is a listing of the major search engines as well as a link for those that offer free submission to their indexes.

www.Ask.com (*at the time of this writing - fee based*)

www.Bing.com (http://www.bing.com/webmaster/SubmitSitePage.aspx)

www.Lycos.com

www.HotBot.com

www. Live.com (*formerly Windows Live Search*)

www.Google.com (http://www.google.com/addurl/)

www.Yahoo.com (www.search.yahoo.com/info/submit.html)

www.GigBlast.com (http://www.gigblast.com/addurl)

www.AltaVista.com (*Powered by Yahoo*)

www.AllTheWeb.com (*Powered by Yahoo*)

www. Search.AOL.com (*AOL search engine*)

www.DuckDuckGo.com

www. Search.Yippy.com (*Yippy*)

www.DogPile.com

www.Exalead.com (http://www.exalead.com/search/)

www.IceRocket.com

www.Teoma.com

www.WebCrawler.com

www.MyWebSearch.com

www.MetaCrawler.com

www.Search.com

www.Mamma.com

www.Go2Net.com

There are entirely too many search engines, directory and metacrawler sites to list here, so by all means don't let this be an all inclusive listing. So do use some of the sites listed above to search for more sites similar to those listed here.

CHAPTER 13
BUSINESS SERVICES WEBSITES

Although, this book was intended to offer a host of free or nearly free resources for helping business owners like you grow your business, I felt compelled to include some additional resources that will aid business owners in this perpetual undertaking.

However, the websites that follow aren't free, but worth every penny in respect to what they can offer your growing business. The following websites are broken up into 3 distinct categories: **Communications**, **Hosting/Web Tools** and **Legal Resources**.

<u>**Communication listings**</u> cover websites that offer such services/products as toll free 800 (*that includes 877, 866, etc.*) numbers for as little as $10 a month to secretarial or phone answering services.

<u>**Hosting/Web Tools listings**</u> cover services which include everything from web hosting to domain name registration to name but a few.

<u>**Legal Resources listings**</u> cover websites that offer a host of legal services as far as business or commercial issues are concerned. Such services include business formation services (*i.e. forming a corporation, LLC, etc.*) to offering ready-made legal or business forms and much more.

Communications

www.PCMSI.com

www.Solutions.LivePerson.com

www.HQ.com

www.YourCityOffice.com

www.GrassHopper.com

www.FreedomVoice.com

www.RingCentral.com

www.Skype.com

www.GoToMeeting.com

www.Microsoft.com *(the link changes so just Google "MS Live Meeting")*

www.ActiveCollab.com

www.CopyCall.com

www.Protus.com

www.TollFreeForwarding.com

www.Vonage.com

www.OneBox.com

www.PhonePeople.com

www.Freedom800.com

Hosting/Web Tools

www.GoDaddy.com

www.HostGator.com

www.HostWay.com

www.ThePlanet.com

www.Brinkster.com

www.1and1.com

www.BlueHost.com

www.HostMonster.com

www.HostGator.com

www.IXWebHosting.com (*www.ixwebhosting.com*)

www.StartLogic.com

www.Google.com (*Google Docs – very useful and free tools*)

www.Checkout.Google.com

www.Mozy.com

www.ZumoDrive.com

www.PayPal.com

www.Authorize.net

www.2Checkout.com

www.FreshBooks.com

www.OpenID.net

www.WorldLingo.com (*offers a website language translator*)

Legal Resources

www.LegalZoom.com

www.FindLegalForms.com

www.MyCorporation.com

www.Nolo.com (*Nolo Press*)

www.USA.gov

www.CopyRight.gov (*US Copyright Office Website*)

www.USPTO.gov (*US Patent & Trademark Office Website*)

CHAPTER 14
SAVY STRATEGIES AND TACTICS

We all know that starting and/or running a business of your own can be very fulfilling and handsomely rewarding. Yet, knowing that "*to whom much is given much is required*", this fulfillment & reward will only be had after much diligence, determination, patience & hard work. In today's ever changing and tight business arena we will need an extra edge or two to ensure our business' success. This section is intended to do just that. In this section I cover some useful strategies, tactics and tips to help you beef up your business in more ways than one.

Image is Everything

One of the greatest factors in a business' success is its' image. Image isn't as narrow as it is often perceived. Image can refer to a number of things including quality, customer service, conflict resolution, etc. A few things you can do particularly as a website owner are as follows:

Make sure you are accessible to your customers/clients. Would you want to do business with someone you can't reach when you need to? Well don't expect your customers/clients to be any different. Being accessible means providing customers/clients with a minimum of two means of contact (*however, the more the better*). Some means of being inexpensively accessible to your customers/clients include (*not all will apply to all, but it is good to have some rather than none at all*):

1. A number (*toll free if you're doing business outside your locale*)

2. Appropriate email addresses (*i.e. sales@mybiz.com, billing@mybiz.com*)

3. A physical address (*particularly so if you are a web only business*)

4. Virtual conferencing (*i.e. Skype, GoToMeeting, Adobe Connect, etc.*)

5. Online chat service (*check out www.LivePerson.com for a great example*)

Another aspect of ensuring your business' image is the way you handle your customers complaints (*if you have any*). Some people can be finicky and as such they will most always speak of the bad or unfavorable experience they had with a business before they will tell of the good. So make sure you handle **ALL** your customers/clients with fragile hands (*figuratively speaking*). Leave no room for complaints (*as much as humanly possible*). One lost customer is one too many.

Marketing & Advertising

Marketing and advertising your business can be challenging considering the numerous avenues available to market and advertise your business, brand, product or service. Then there is the often high cost of marketing and advertising that also is a factor in deciding when, where and how to market and advertise your business.

Contrary to popular propaganda there is no one method to successful marketing and advertising. There are various combinations of avenue, cost and targeting. What the right combination is depends on a variety of factors, particularly the product/service, expense budget and your intended target. With that said, I am going to use the following pages to illustrate some tactful methods and strategies for getting the word about your business, brand, product, service, idea or opportunity.

The Best of Both Worlds

One aspect of successful marketing for any business particularly those website only businesses involves the use of both online and offline marketing and advertising. Many times as a website [only] business, all too often many owners exhaust there efforts on "online only" campaigns.

This is a very bad approach or way of thinking for several distinct factors: Although, many people spend hours at a time online, consider that the average person works 8 + hours a day at least 5 days a week, not to mention they often spend there "outside of work" hours also away from the computer (*i.e. commuting to & from, dining out, outdoor entertainment, shopping, family time, news/TV watching, etc.*). So thinking that you'll gain all of your audience from online marketing/advertising alone is a flawed and ineffective approach. Yes, there are many examples of websites that have been successful by online only marketing and advertising, but believe me they are far and few in between the millions of other websites who failed trying this method. Yes by all means use online marketing/advertising to your advantage but also incorporate some offline input as well, this makes for a well balanced marketing and advertising regime.

The world of online marketing and advertising although very much conquerable can be daunting, challenging and tedious. Don't get me wrong, SEO services as mentioned earlier in this book can play a vital role in your overall marketing and advertising efforts. But there are a few overrated and often misleading concepts about SEO services, that we need to start weaning ourselves away from or off of.

At the top of the misconception list is the notion of popping up at the number one spot in search results. Although very much possible (*particularly if the searcher specifically puts in the exact or similar name of your business/website*), it is not likely for the average website owner. Why? Well think about just how ridicules this notion of every one of us who own a web site in a given industry popping up at the number one spot or even on the first page of search results is? It is mathematically impossible for all of us to be first on the list. Also consider that in any given industry they are virtually thousands (*and in some cases millions*) of websites boasting the same or similar related products and/or services of that particular industry.

And unless you have Google, MSN or Yahoo money you are not likely to come close to being first. Besides, if you had this kind of money obviously your marketing and advertising efforts are proving their worth and you'd have little to no need for this book. Again, SEO services are genuinely beneficial.

But they should be approached with realistic perceptions as well expectations. By this I mean, know that such services will not necessarily place you at the number one spot but will however make your website more search engine friendly which can never be a bad thing. And if you do happen to dominate a particular region, state, city or locale good meta tag info (*i.e. keywords, page descriptions, etc.*) in your web pages can prove beneficial as well.

So the best approach among others to prevailing online is two-fold. On the one hand online success is a matter of being (*or being mentioned*) in as many different places (*on the web*) inexpensively as possible (*hint: use the sites listed in the previous pages wisely and by all means aggressively to do just that*).

On the other hand, prevailing online is also a matter of using offline marketing and advertising alongside your online efforts. This includes when possible publications (*i.e. magazines, newspapers, etc.*), outdoor (*i.e. billboards, digital signage displays, mobile ads, etc.*), television/radio as well as direct mail efforts.

With that said, let me illustrate several approaches to marketing and advertising that can help you rapidly spread the word about your business, brand, product, service, idea or opportunity.

Online Marketing/Advertising

Although I have listed numerous websites in the previous pages that are all geared toward helping you promote for little to no cost, I would also like to add a few tips for making the most of your online efforts.

Customer's Love Incentives:

First I would like to advice you to offer incentives for customers if they become friends, contacts, etc. on some of your accounts to some of the networking websites listed earlier. An example would be to give customers say a 1 - 5% discount if they become a contact on your facebook page or join your linkedin network, etc. This will not only put your brand business, product, service, idea or opportunity in front of all the contacts they have it will also beef up your brand following.

Compliments are Always Welcomed:

Next find websites that offer complimentary products/services to your own (*non-competitive*) and offer to put a link to their site on your website in exchange for a link of your website on theirs. Similar to link exchanges, but more personal, since you will be doing it yourself.

Email Marketing Made Simple:

Also be sure to utilize email marketing in your online campaigns. Although, many of us aren't tidy when it comes to keeping our inbox messages to a minimum, email marketing can still prove well worth the effort. Consider this, for less than $20 you can send out as many as 5000 opt-in emails to prospects a month. The key elements to successful email marketing is being consistent, practical and most certainly ethical. **DO NOT** spam (*send unsolicited emails*), set a budget to send out a certain amount of opt-in emails a month and stick with that plan rain, sleet, hail or snow, so to speak. Start small and grow as your results start to grow. (**see pg 21**)

Press Releases The E-Way:

Another useful tactic is online press releases. Because many of the websites who offer online press release services can often put your message in front of a lot readers who may have an interest in your pitch. Most even offer their services as free/self serve. Remember its about being in as many places on the web as possible. (**see pg 23**)

Yellow - The Color of Exposure:

Simple but effective. It pays to get listed with The Yellow Pages (*both online and offline versions*). They can often put you/your company in the reach of thousands of local searchers. (see **www.YellowBook.com** for details)

Let me say that the aforementioned tactics for online promoting isn't an end all list, but merely a starting point for you to experiment and incorporate other tactics to do with.

Offline Marketing/Advertising

The beauty of offline marketing and advertising is that is offers more avenues than online does. It also can wet the whistle of your prospects to buy lacing them with just enough info about your business, brand, product, service, idea or opportunity to make them go seek you out online.

Contrary to popular belief, this young grasshopper is the key to building traffic to your website. Although its not overnight when they start coming from offline means searching specifically for your website and as enough people start do it then your brand becomes entrenched in the search engines for being searched so frequently. Couple this with your online efforts and it can be hard for your business to not be noticed!

Be Direct to Your Prospects:

Direct mail is not only multi-dimensional its a very powerful means of marketing your business. It can involve postcard marketing, inserts (*i.e. having a pamphlet, booklet, flyer, etc. inserted into a newspaper, magazine, mailing etc.*) passing out of business cards, brochures, door hangers etc. Make no mistake about it the potential of direct mail is diverse and powerful.

Treat your postcard marketing efforts just as I spoke of about email marketing (*start small and with a budget, but be aggressively consistent*). The following companies offer postcard marketing, mailing lists and/or direct mailing services among others:

www.VistaPrint.com (*also offers low cost printing services*)

www.InfoUSA.com

www.DirectMail.com

www.Valassis.com (*formerly Advo*)

www.AmazingMail.com

www.ModernPostcard.com

www.ListAssociates.net

www.MailingLists.com

www.ResponseMail.com

www.USPSEveryDoor.com (*a powerful service offered by the US Postal Service*)

As far as the other methods of direct mail use them according to your needs and means. Some good advice though, you can never have enough business cards, brochures and door hangers. They come cheap but are priceless on always having you prepared to spread the word about your promotions. So let me say it again, "**YOU CAN NEVER HAVE TOO MANY BUSINESS CARDS, BROCHURES and DOOR HANGERS**".

It's All in The Print:

Another slept on means of inexpensively (*in respect to the reach that can be had*) of marketing/advertising is through the use of relevant (*and in some cases not so relevant*) publications. This can include (*but definitely not be limited to*) daily or weekly newspapers, magazines, penny savers, coupon books, etc. Some of these publications can be expensive but well worth the cost, while others can be cheap but just as effective.

One particularly powerful means, but rarely known method that I have been using for years with great results is through the use of newspaper associations. See most papers in any given state belong to that states press association. And as a result (*I believe because the internet has been dipping into newspapers advertising revenue pot also*) these associations offer a powerful ad service. For one set price they will place a classified ad, 2" x 2" display ad or 2" x 4" display ad (*not all offer the classified or 2" x 4"*) in every newspaper that belongs to its association in their state. Talk about exposure . . . Doesn't get any better!

SOME EXAMPLES:

The Illinois Press Association offers a 2" x 2" display ad in as many as 257 different newspaper with a total circulation of 1.1 million + for $1,499.00.

The Kansas Press Association offers a 2" x 2" display ad in as many as 144 different newspaper with a total circulation of 410,000 + for $899.00.

The Wyoming Press Association offers a 2" x 2" display ad in as many as 43 different newspaper with a total circulation of 175,000 for $579.00.

Keep in mind also that circulation is modest, considering the fact that it doesn't by any means convey true viewership. This is primarily because many papers are viewed by multiple persons (*i.e. at the library, spas, fitness centers, same house hold, lobbies, etc.*), so your ad buy will literally reach across a given state. Not a bad exchange!

For your complete convenience I have provided a complete listing of all state's prices, circulations and number of participating newspapers on the following pages.

I have also provided a listing of all participating state's website addresses at the end of the listing of prices, circulation figures and the number of participating newspapers for each state.

NOTE: I have tried to be as accurate as possible in the following listings. However, the prices, circulation figures and/or number of participating newspapers may have changed since the initial publishing of this book.

State	Ad Size	Cost	Circulation	Num. of Newspapers
Alabama	2 x 2	$1099.00	725,000	114
Alaska	1 x 2	$789.00	270,000	19
Arizona	2 x 2	$798.00	720,341	63
Arkansas	2 x 2	$1249.00	1,074,242	124
California	2 x 2	$1599.00	1,500,000	140
Colorado	2 x 2	$949.00	418,178	80
Florida	2 x 2	$1359.00	1,190,146	94
Georgia	2 x 2	$1499.00	811,272	90

State	Ad Size	Cost	Circulation	Num. of Newspapers
Hawaii	2 x 2	$1584.00	731,000	14
Illinois	2 x 2	$1499.00	1,194,022	257
Indiana	2 x 2	$999.00	760,000	63
Iowa	2 x 2	$1299.00	905,000	213
Kansas	2 x 2	$899.00	410,783	144
Kentucky	2 x 2	$2367.00	957,105	98
Louisiana	2 x 2	$749.00	460,000	67
MDDC*	2 x 2	$1549.00	2,000,000	100

*MDDC represents Maryland, Delaware and The District of Columbia (DC) combined.

State	Ad Size	Cost	Circulation	Num. of Newspapers
Michigan	2 x 2	$1098.00	1,320,000	113
Minnesota	2 x 2	$1899.00	1,015,000	264
Mississippi	2 x 2	$1149.00	1,001,851	93
Missouri	2 x 2	$1099.00	866,215	157
Montana	2 x 2	$459.00	150,166	49
Nebraska	2 x 2	$924.00	377,841	171
N. England*	2 x 2	$2048.00	1,402,111	127

*New England represents Connecticut, Maine, Massachusetts, New Hampshire, Rhode Island and Vermont.

State	Ad Size	Cost	Circulation	Num. of Newspapers
New Jersey	2 x 2	$1294.00	1,500,000	140
N. Mexico	2 x 2	$899.00	205,419	28
New York	2 x 2	$2898.00	2,622,979	300
Nevada	2 x 2	$789.00	396,973	20
N. Carolina	2 x 2	$1499.00	1,335,502	74
N. Dakota	2 x 2	$599.00	300,000	90
Ohio	2 x 2	$949.00	705,275	65
Oklahoma	2 x 2	$2599.00	507,997	182
Oregon	2 x 2	$749.00	387,063	56

State	Ad Size	Cost	Circulation	Num. of Newspapers
Pennsylvania	2 x 2	$1449.00	1,200,000	93
S. Carolina	2 x 2	$1699.00	1,251,152	103
S. Dakota	2 x 2	$899.00	299,200	128
Tennessee	2 x 2	$1134.00	579,214	81
Texas	2 x 2	$1199.00	712,376	243
Utah	2 x 2	$414.00	200,000	40
Virginia	2 x 2	$1049.00	1,011,427	71
Washington	2 x 2	$1049.00	764,519	75

State	Ad Size	Cost	Circulation	Num. of Newspapers
W. Virginia	2 x 2	$699.00	534,527	51
Wisconsin	2 x 2	$1449.00	945,700	150
Wyoming	2 x 2	$579.00	175,000	43

Newspaper Associations' Website Addresses:

Alabama (www.alabamapress.org)

Arizona (www.ananews.com)

Arkansas (www.arkansaspress.org)

California (www.cnpa.com)

Colorado (www.coloradopressassociation.com)

Florida (www.flpress.com)

Georgia (www.gapress.org)

Indiana (www.gapress.org)

Idaho (www.idahopressclub.org)

Illinois (www.il-press.com)

Iowa (www.inanews.com)

Kansas (www.kspress.com)

Kentucky (www.kypress.com)

Louisiana (www.lapress.com)

Michigan (www.michiganpress.org)

Minnesota (www.mnnewspapernet.org)

Mississippi (www.mspress.org)

Missouri (www.mopress.com)

Montana (www.mtnewspapers.com)

Nebraska (www.nebpress.com)

New England (www.nenpa.com)

New Jersey (www.njpa.org)

New York (www.nynpa.com) (www.nynewspapers.com)

North Carolina (www.ncpress.com)

North Dakota (www.ndna.com)

Ohio (www.ohionews.org)

Oklahoma (www.ohionews.org)

Oregon (www.orenews.com)

Pennsylvania (www.pa-newspaper.org)

South Carolina (www.scpress.org)

South Dakota (www.sdna.com)

Some Independent Southern States (www.snpa.org)

Suburban Newspapers of America (www.suburban-news.org)

Tennessee (www.tnpress.com)

Texas (www.texaspress.com)

Texas Dailies (www.tdna.org)

Utah (www.utahpress.com)

Virginia (www.vpa.net)

Washington (www.wnpa.com)

West Virginia (www.wvpress.org)

Wisconsin (www.wnanews.com)

Wyoming (www.wyopress.org)

As you can see with these buys there is room for you to powerfully and effectively spread the word about your promotion. Contact any of the state's associations for complete details about these buys.

I have also chosen to list several more websites related to newspaper marketing and advertising that I thought would benefit you as they have me. They are as follows:

www.Jigsaw.com

www.GebbieInc.com (*sales listings or directories of magazines, newspapers, etc.*)

www.AmmClas.com

I have just a few more tidbits to lay on you before I let you go, so bear with me young grasshopper, I'm not done with you yet.

Getting Out:

Another powerful method of marketing and advertising that's very effective but tends to often be expensive is outdoor advertising. Essentially outdoor advertising includes billboards, mobile ads (*i.e. on the side of trucks, cabs, etc.*), digital display signs, etc.

As I've stated although most of these ads can be expensive, they are never the less definitely worth mentioning and when you're able to, utilizing. So when you graduate to the big leagues these outdoor companies/websites will come in handy:

www.AdamsOutdoor.com

www.ClearChannel.com

www.HicksOutdoor.com

www.TitanOutdoor.com

Although there are plenty other players in the outdoor arena, the above can get you started in that direction.

Get The Picture:

Another powerful and yes, often expensive (*but not as expensive as many people may think*) is television advertising. Although the dynamics of television advertising could make for a complete book unto itself, I will not waste your time covering the gargantuan avenues to get your message on the big screen, I will use this section to mention a lesser known but very effective means of getting your ad on television.

The internet has brought about automation for everything from ordering products to making online reservation to . . . yep you guessed it, ordering television ad space online. There is a little known company called Spot

Runner (www.spotrunner.com) that offers such a unique spin on television advertising. They even offer the ability for you to use pre-made commercials all you have to do is punch in your own content as far as website address, phone number, etc. then you simply pick the channels (i.e. CNN, Disney Network, TBS, etc.) and BAM your ready to hit the big screen. What's even more convenient is you can do all this from within your account panel, how snazzy is that!

Some other useful websites for television and/or video promotions are as follows:

www.SpotMixer.com

www.ThoughtEquity.com

www.Admira.navic.tv

Well young grasshopper there you have it! An arsenal of marketing and advertising tips, strategies and resources at your disposal. I wish you all the best in all your endeavors. On a parting note I would like to offer a few things about becoming and staying on the path of success. Keep these in mind when pursuing your dreams of business ownership and financial freedom.

1. Know that success is not a destination, but more of an ongoing journey.

2. Consistency overcomes poor results.

3. Frustration is your enemy . . . So keep your distance from it at all cost!

4. Patience, Persistence and Perseverance will be your most valuable assets.

YOU CAN AND WILL ACHIEVE WHAT YOU SET OUT TOO!

JUST <u>NEVER</u> GIVE UP! SEE YOU AT THE TOP!

ABOUT THE AUTHOR

Between studying for exams, Corwin spends much of his time in self study, designing websites, logos as well as many other designs for a host of clients creating and maintaining some of his own projects, reading (*IT books of course*), exercising, amateur martial arts, sharpening his pool game and playing chess.